FIRENZE
MVSEI

National Museum of the Bargello

Giovanna Gaeta Bertelà

GIUNTI

*Updated text
and entries (pp. 27, 31, 73, 76)*
Maria Grazia Vaccari

Graphic design: Franco Bulletti
Cover design: Laura Belforte *and* Fabio Filippi
Floor plans: Fabio Filippi *and* Paola Zacchini

Editorial manager: Claudio Pescio
Editing: Augusta Tosone
Translation: Helen Cleary, Helen Glave, *and* Joan M. Reifsnyder

Photos: National Museum of the Bargello, Giunti Archive,
Antonio Quattrone, Rabatti & Domingie Photography - Florence

www. giunti.it

First edition: February 1999
Second edition revised: February 2005

Editorial production of Giunti Editore S.p.A., Florence-Milan

Reprint	Year
5 4 3 2 1	2009 2008 2007 2006

Printed by Giunti Industrie Grafiche S.p.A. – Prato

CONTENTS

The medieval *Lion* in the Courtyard

*E*NOUGH BOOKS *have been written about the public museums in Florence run by the Soprintendenza per il Polo Museale Fiorentino to fill a large library. This is hardly surprising when one considers that the artistic heritage preserved in our museums has been famous throughout the world for centuries. For hundreds of years writers, scholars and travellers of every nationality and country have been attempting to describe all that the Florentine museums contain. They have made great efforts to explain why these museums are so fascinating, and to lead a path through paintings and sculptures for both the uninformed but willing visitor and the refined and exacting intellectual.*

Over time, however, the museums have altered their aspect and their layout, the exhibitions have been arranged in new ways, the collections have been enriched (or impoverished). Attributions of works in the museums have also changed, restorations have transformed the appearance of many pieces, the rise and fall of aesthetic tendencies have led to reorganisation and the exhibition of differing works. All these things are constantly taking place within the public collections because the museology and the history of art, like any intellectual endeavour, are in a constant state of progress and transformation. This explains why the literature surrounding the Florentine museums (like that of any of the world's great art collections) is so immense, and in a process of continual updating and change.

The perfect, definitive guide to a museum, any museum, does not and cannot exist.

The premise seems obvious, but is nonetheless necessary in order to understand the point of the publication introduced by these lines. From the moment when, in accordance with the application of the Ronchey law 4/93, the Giunti publishing house group took over the running of the support services within the Florentine museum system, it was decided to start at once on a standardised series of illustrated guides. These guides, displaying the cuneiform flower of "Firenze Musei" on the cover, guarantee that at the year of publication the state of each museum is exactly that described in the guide.

Certain things are obviously necessary if a museum guide is to aspire to reliability, official standing and at the same time enjoy a wide distribution: accuracy of information, high quality reproductions, an easily manageable format, a reasonable cost and – not least – a clearly written text (without, naturally, being banal or lacking in precision). Readers will judge for themselves if the guide which follows this introduction reaches these standards. I have no doubt that this will be a serious and committed judgement, just as myself and the Publisher of this guide have been serious and committed in attempting to meet the cultural needs of whoever visits our museums in the best way and with every possible care.

The Superintendent
for Polo Museale Fiorentino
(Antonio Paolucci)

ANDRÉ DURAN, *The Courtyard of the Bargello used as a public prison*

THE NATIONAL MUSEUM OF THE BARGELLO

THE HISTORY OF THE NATIONAL MUSEUM of the Bargello is intrinsically linked to that of the Palazzo, one of the oldest public buildings in Florence, in which it has been housed since its foundation in 1865. According to Vasari the Palazzo Pretorio (later the Palazzo of the Bargello) was built for the Captain of the People by Lapo Tedesco, Arnolfo di Cambio's father and maestro. It was begun in the mid-thirteenth century, during the years when the great basilicas of Florence were being planned, in the area overlooking Via del Proconsolo, on the site of houses and towers belonging to the church of the Badia. It was later extended over the Via dell'Acqua, completed by a severe internal courtyard, and enhanced by the addition of Gothic features such as double and single arched windows and battlements. It became the seat of the Podestà and played a crucial role in the historical events of the city. As well as suffering many natural disasters such as fires and floods, the building was also the scene of popular riots. In 1434 Cosimo the Elder decreed that the figures of the hanged Florentine nobles who had opposed his return be painted on the façade, and in 1480 members of the Pazzi family were depicted there by Andrea del Castagno. From 1502 to 1574 it was the seat of the Council of Justice and the Magistrates of the "Ruota", after which it was taken over by the Captain of Justice known as the "Bargello" and was made over into a city prison. From this time on, the neglect and squalor became increasingly marked: the rooms were disfigured and the arches of the Verone (Loggia) and the Courtyard were walled in, while numerous mezzanine floors were constructed to serve as prison cells, completely distorting the original structure of the Palace. Even the large hall on the first floor where the meetings of the Council had been held, now the Donatello Hall, was sub-divided into thirty-two cells arranged in four rows and a chapel. The Chapel of St Mary Magdalene itself, the artistic and historical fulcrum of the building, was plastered over and separated into two floors, with the upper level allocated to the prison and the lower to a storeroom. Only during the nineteenth century, erudite interest in the glories of the city and the indication of the presence of Giotto's *Portrait of Dante* in the Magdalene's Chapel, reawakened positive interest in the Palazzo del Podestà and in its restoration.

In the 1840s the recuperation in the Bargello Chapel of the *Portrait of Dante*, and the discovery of the wall frescoes (*Paradise*, *Stories of Our Lady's Flight into Egypt and of the life of Mary Magdalene, Hell*) which according to Vasari are by Giotto, led to a greater appreciation of the Palazzo, resulting in its deserved, though slow, restoration. The image of the divine poet, which circulated in prints, was reproduced in Italian and foreign reviews and mentioned in guidebooks and manuals, thus contributing to the fame of the Chapel and consequently to that of the monumental Palace itself. On the occasion of the transfer of the Italian Capital to Florence (1865-1871), it was decided to restore the Bargello, which assumed a very specific role within the prevailing neo-Gothic climate and the nineteenth-century Romantic debate. Francesco Mazzei, architect of the Royal Manufactures with proven experience in Volterra and in the Florentine State Archives, was commissioned to carry out the work. Contemporary prints and Mazzei's report bear witness to the serious state of dilapidation: 'The loggia was disfigured and closed in by walls without any consideration for the stonework or the solidity. On three sides the courtyard was blocked in by a vast portico of blackened columns... on the west side projected a wide staircase leaning against the outer wall of the courtyard, with a landing and doorway space half way up... leading on the right into the prisons adjacent to the vast hall... The walls of this façade of the courtyard, as well as the wall sections between the arches were covered with the coats-of-arms of the Podestà and the Magistrates of the Ruota, all of which together lent and still lend this Palace a most formidable appearance of power and terror, enough to make even the most cheerful thoughts gloomy'. In 1861, on the occasion of the First Italian National Exhibition, the Palace 'was entirely cleared... and it was possible to show to the public the parts of the building which had already been

Detail of the Courtyard, with a glimpse of the Verone (Loggia)

restored'. The work, which was taken up again after the Exhibition, 'consist-ed... in the completion of the second [inner] staircase. [The tower] was rebuilt on the Via Ghibellina side, and to avoid any visual impression of overhanging, it was decided to rusticate the façade, like that of the part overlooking the old church of the Badia'.

The Loggia too was restored and the fountain, situated on the corner be-tween Via del Proconsolo and Via della Vigna Vecchia, was moved to the in-side. To embellish the courtyard it was decided to destroy the roof protecting the staircase and to introduce an iron gateway half way up, to build a well (in the place of the legendary scaffold) and to repave the flint courtyard with bricks laid in a herringbone pattern. The decoration of the area was also taken in hand, and entrusted to Carlo Brazzini and Gaetano Bianchi. The plan for the pictorial design of the Courtyard was to represent, among other things, 'the coats-of-arms of the four city *quartieri*... and of the sixteen *gonfaloni* or armed companies of the people'. The painted arms were to be flanked by stone es-cutcheons, partially derived from similar Tuscan monuments. The entire restoration was terminated in 1865 after 'much meticulous study so that every-thing should correspond to the age of the building'. The reorganisation of this glorious Palazzo, with its prestigious role in Florentine history, required lengthy debate and reflection. Following the French example of Alexandre Lenoir's Musée des Monuments, the Royal Decree of 1859 destined 'the Palagio del Podestà... to be the seat of a Museum of ancient monuments, through which, and in whatever manner, the history of Tuscany should be illustrated in every-thing relating to institutions, traditions and arts'. In this way the Bargello would have brought together objects representative of different periods, materials and techniques which were essential to a historical appreciation of Tuscan civilisation. The project was subjected to numerous modifications, with pro-posals for a Museum of Industrial Arts, a Medieval Museum, and a National Historical Archaeological Museum, until finally, on 22 June 1865, the present title of the National Museum was decided upon.

The opening of the Museum to the public (with a heterogeneous range of exhibits, including collections from the Uffizi Gallery, sculptures from the Roy-al Manufactures and the suppressed monasteries, and objects deposited by private collectors) was marked by a celebration of Dante. Just as it had been crucial for the restoration of the building, the name of the poet constituted the essential link between the history of the Palazzo and the nascent Museum. Open on the ground floor were two rooms arranged for the exhibition of ar-mour and one for sculpture, while on the first floor was the large hall display-ing monumental sculptures (including Michelangelo's *Vittoria*) from the Sa-lone dei Cinquecento in the Palazzo Vecchio. These were soon to be augmented by varied examples of the "minor" arts, supplied by private loan and donation, as well as by the Uffizi Gallery. These included majolica ware, waxworks, enamels, sacred and secular jewellery, ivories, chests, amberware, bronze statuary, Renaissance sculptures (including works by Donatello and Michelan-gelo), terracottas, tapestries, furniture, medals, seals and textiles. In 1875 Pasquale Villari emphasised the need for the establishment of an artistic-industrial school at the Bargello, in a 'Museum for which everyone envies us'. The Donatello celebrations of 1887 in the large hall on the first floor favoured instead the creation of a Donatello Tribuna, and marked the initial and definitive layout of the Renaissance sculpture. This large first-floor hall was set aside for those of Donatello's works which were already in the Museum: the *Marzocco*, the *Atys*, the bronze and marble *Davids*, the *St John the Baptist*, the bust of *Niccolò da Uzzano*, while among those which came from outside the Museum, were the *Hilt* (from the Armoury of Turin), the marble busts of the *Vanchetonis*, and the plaster casts of the *Gattamelata*, and of numerous sculptures from the altar of the St Anthony in Padua. Worthy companion pieces to these works were provided by the loans from lay organisations, antiquarians and collectors (among them Stefano Bardini, Louis Carrand, Giulio Franchetti, and Vincenzo Funghini) with a range of sacred and secular objects distributed throughout the other rooms. Nevertheless, the true character of the Museum was not definitively established until the following year, in 1888, with the bequest of the Carrand collection of Gothic and Renaissance objects. Byzantine and early medieval ivories, French and Islamic Gothic ivories, Limoges enamels dating from the thirteenth to the sixteenth century, precious stones, cameos, sacred and secular jewellery, Islamic and Indian metalwork, skins, precious textiles, engraved woodwork, paste caskets, majolica ware, glassware, and bronzes; the legacy of the Lyon collector Louis Carrand formed the first real nucleus of the National Museum's "minor" arts collection. Like the Museum of Cluny, through the receipt of this heterogeneous collection of exemplars of varied character – which was later to be augmented by the Ressman collection of armoury and the Franchetti collection of early and Renaissance textiles – the Bargello acquired an international *status* in the realm of the "minor arts" similar to the level it had already reached in the sphere of Renaissance sculpture. At the end of the nineteenth century, the Uffizi, which was gradually becoming defined as a treasure-house of ancient masterpieces and particularly as a picture-gallery, made a further transfer to the Bargello of its collection of plaques and most of the Medici medals. In 1903 in his *Italian Diary* Hermann Hesse described the National Museum, pausing on the works of Michelangelo, but also praising the 'Courtyard with its elegant staircase and gallery decorated with many coats-of-arms, the whole ingenuous, spare and succinct, yet at the same time celebratory and aggressive'. Similarly, he praised the Donatello Room 'decidedly serious and dignified', the 'rich collection of minor art', the ivories, the medals, and, among the bronzes, Verrocchio's *David*. Giacomo De Nicola's idea of reorganising the Carrand, Ressman and Franchetti bequests by transferring them into the large hall, and moving Donatello's works into the present Baroque Sculpture and Medals Rooms, was fortunately not carried through. Since then the Bargello, like a well-filled coffer, has housed the plastic masterpieces of the Renaissance and of the 'arts related to those of the Guilds', pursuing its function as museum through the constant enrichment of the collections thanks to the generous contributions of private individuals and specific state purchases, in the profound and indivisible union of container (the Palazzo) and contents (the sculptures and objects).

External view of the Bargello

THE MICHELANGELO ROOM

In the nineteenth-century layout this room, decorated by Gaetano Bianchi, was designed as a picturesque background for the collection of armoury. After the flood of 1966, it was restored and repainted (only a fresco from the School of Giotto depicting the Virgin and Child, *restored in 2001, now remains) and allocated to the display of the most prestigious examples of sixteenth-century sculpture, many of which came to the Bargello in the 1870's from the Uffizi Gallery. Selected to accompany the works of Michelangelo (*Pitti Tondo, David-Apollo, Brutus *and* Bacchus*) in the current exhibition are: Giovan Francesco Rustici's* Tondo, *Iacopo Sansovino's* Bacchus *(which previously adorned the chamber of Cosimo I in the Palazzo Vecchio, together with Buonarroti's* David-Apollo *and Baccio Bandinelli's* Bacchus*), works by Benvenuto Cellini (the marble base for the* Perseus, *the relief with the* Liberation of Andromeda, *wax and bronze models for the* Perseus, Narcissus*) and by Bandinelli (*Bust of Cosimo I, Adam and Eve*), Vincenzo Danti (*Honour overcoming Deceit*), Bartolomeo Ammannati (*Nari Tomb*) and Giambologna (*Florence subduing Pisa, Mercury, *previously at the Villa Medici at Pincio).*

**MICHELANGELO
BUONARROTI**
Bacchus
(with detail)

1496-1497
Marble
Height 207
Sculpture Inv. no. 10

In 1496 Cardinal Raffaello Sansoni Riario commissioned from the young Michelangelo during his first Roman sojourn, a statue of *Bacchus*, which was completed the following year. The statue, which was intended for the decoration of the Palazzo della Cancelleria, did not meet with the Cardinal's approval, and he sold it to the banker Iacopo Galli who placed it in the garden of his residence. The fame of the work, which was drawn by Martin van Heemskerck and by Cornelis Bos (1533-1538) and consecrated in Vasari's *Lives*, contributed in 1570-1571 to its purchase, through Diomede Leoni, by the Medici family who transferred it to the Uffizi. Here in 1591 it was seen by Bocchi who praised 'The bodily form delicate and yet gracefully swift, with a beauty from every aspect that demands an incomparable artistry'; in 1871 the statue came to the Bargello.

**MICHELANGELO
BUONARROTI**
*Madonna and Child
with the Infant St John
(Pitti Tondo)*
(with detail)

1504-1505
Marble
Diameter 80
Sculpture Inv. no. 93

In 1823 the Lorraine government bought the *Pitti Tondo* from the antiquarian Fedele Acciai for the Uffizi Gallery. In 1873 it passed to the Bargello, where it was placed, together with the *Bacchus*, the *David -Apollo* and the *Brutus* in a minor gallery (at present given over to temporary exhibitions). A work from Michelangelo's youthful period, it is mentioned by Giorgio Vasari in the biography of the artist who 'in this same period [1504] roughed out and did not finish two marble medallions, one for Taddeo Taddei, now in his house, and the other for Bartolomeo Pitti, which was given by Fra Miniato Pitti of Monte Oliveto... to Luigi Guicciardini'.

A work dating to the years between the marble *David* in the Accademia Gallery and the Sistine Chapel frescoes,

the *Pitti Tondo* reveals the progressive abandonment of distinct outlines and the gradual and subtle approach to chiaroscuro effects. The private commissioning and the domestic devotional role did not further the fame and reputation of the work, which remained practically unknown until the early years of the 19th century.

15

MICHELANGELO BUONARROTI
David-Apollo
(with detail)

1530-1532
Marble
Height 147
Sculpture Inv. no. 121

The statue was commissioned from Michelangelo by the Medici governor, as confirmed by Vasari in his *Lives*: '[Michelangelo]... began another marble statue for Baccio Valori, of an Apollo extracting an arrow from his quiver, so that it might be a means in his favour of making peace with the Pope and with the house of the Medici, which had been greatly offended by him'.

And in 1531 Valori himself wrote to the artist: 'I do not wish to solicit you regarding my statue, because I am most certain that the affection which I know you bear me has no need of solicitude. I would remind you that, for the satisfaction of my soul, there is nothing that I desire more than this'.

In 1531 Clement VII issued a brief in which he enjoined the artist to work exclusively for him. In the 1568 edition Vasari again mentions: 'To gain the friendship of Baccio

Valori, Michelangelo began a six-feet high marble figure of an Apollo withdrawing an arrow from his quiver, bringing it almost to completion; this is now in the hall of the Prince of Florence, which is a most singular occurrence, considering that it is not completely finished'.

Effectively, the Medici Inventory of 1553 mentions the statue in the chamber of Cosimo I in the Palazzo Vecchio. Subsequently, up until 1824, it was relegated to the amphitheatre at Boboli, after which it was transferred to the Uffizi Gallery and positioned opposite the *Bacchus* in the west corridor.

From here, in the eighteen-seventies it passed to the Bargello, with all its problems of chronology, interpretation (the head of Goliath under the foot, the bow in the rough section behind the shoulders, stone in the right hand) and morality (conqueror and conquered according to Baccio Valori, in the symbolic representation of the Biblical hero tackling the giant).

In its calibrated rhythms and cadenced and asymmetrical movement, the figure seems to belong with the dynamic classicism of the *Allegories* of the New Sacristy.

MICHELANGELO BUONARROTI
Brutus
(with detail)

1539-1540
Marble
Height 96
Sculpture Inv. no. 97

The bust was commissioned from Michelangelo by his friend Cardinal Ridolfi through Donato Giannotti, both of whom were exponents of the anti-Medici party, as a justification (through the example of Caesar's murderer) of the assassination in 1537 of Duke Alexander de' Medici, oppressor of Florentine freedom, on the part of Lorenzo de' Medici. To avoid any political reference, Vasari referred the design of the bust to a purely classical inspiration, 'a head of Brutus in marble, with bust, considerably larger than life-size... performed through the most minute chiselling. This [Michelangelo] had taken from a portrait of the same Brutus engraved in a cornelian cameo... very ancient, which is a most rare object'. The bust proves to have been bought in 1590 by the Grand Duke Ferdinand I from the heirs of Diomede Leoni for the Villa of Petraia, from where it was transferred to the Uffizi Gallery. This "unfinished" work was promptly reflected in the preparatory studies for the contemporary frescoes of the *Sistine Judgement*. Tiberio Calcagni's additions in the drapery and on part of the neck were marginal.

19

Benvenuto Cellini, *Danaë and the Young Perseus*,
detail of the base of the *Perseus*

BENVENUTO CELLINI
Base of the "Perseus"
(details of the niches)
1545-1554
Greek marble and bronze
Height 213
Sculpture Inv. no. 531;
Bronzes nos. 818-822
From the Loggia dei Lanzi
in Piazza della Signoria (2000)

After its restoration in 2000, the base of the *Perseus* was transferred to the Bargello for conservation reasons. The small bronze statues from the niches in the base have been housed in the Bargello since 1971, where the bas-relief depicting the *Liberation of Andromeda* has been since the 1930s. The bronze sculpture itself remains in the Piazza della Signoria under the Loggia dei Lanzi, standing on a copy of the marble base, decorated by copies of the bronze niche sculptures and the relief with An-

dromeda. The commission of the monumental statue by Cosimo I was part of the program publicly affirming Medici power. The Duke himself chose the subject from Ovid's *Metamorphoses*. The realisation of the work was long in coming due to the complex conceptual elaboration, as well as to the technical difficulties in casting a richly detailed statue measuring over three metres high. There were two models made during the planning phase, one in wax and the other in bronze, both in the Bargello Museum. The theme for the marble base centres on the divine protection for Perseus' undertakings. The four niches house bronze statuettes of *Danaë and the Young Perseus* her son, his father *Jupiter*, and his siblings *Miner-*

va and *Mercury*, all identified by Benedetto Varchi's inscriptions. Even though the marble is deteriorated after centuries outdoors, the exuberant, very refined sculpted decoration is still highly effectual. The base is conceived as a pagan altar with four caprine heads on the four corners. These are interpreted as a reference to the constellation of Capricorn, the ascendant of Cosimo I. Four corner figures depicting Diana of Ephesus, an allegorical representation of nature, are found on the lower register. Above the niches on each side there are masks with long beards, their curls artfully arranged, mouths open and eyes filled with terror. The sculptor also worked with collaborators on the piece, and in particular, Francesco del Tadda.

THE IVORIES ROOM

In the 19th century this room housed ivory exhibits from the Medici collections, which were later transferred to the Museo degli Argenti. The nucleus of the collection on display was bequeathed to the Museum in 1888 by Louis Carrand: diptychs, plaquettes, mirror-cases, pastoral staffs, caskets, combs, hunting horns and statuettes reveal the variety of uses of this precious material which was as sought-after as gold or silver, and provide an exceptional illustration of microsculpture in ivory from the 5th to the 15th century. From Byzantium the use of ivory spread between the 8th and the 9th century to the court of Charlemagne and was particularly popular in France during the Gothic period. Alongside the ivories, the current exhibition displays objects made of other materials with similar characteristics and purposes. On the walls are polychrome wooden sculptures from the 13th to the 15th century (Sainted Bishop, Enthroned Madonna and Child, Madonna and Child with St Anne, St Barbara) and two rare mosaics (Pantocrator from the mid-12th century and St Peter from Domenico Ghirlandaio's workshop).

ITALIAN ART
Diptych of Adam and St Paul
(detail with *Adam*)

Late 4th, early 5th century

Elephant ivory
29.6×12.7
Carrand Inv. no. 19

This exceptional diptych came to the Museum with the Louis Carrand Collection, but was probably purchased in Lyons by his father Jean Baptiste in the early 19th century; it is one of the most important pieces of the collection. It is composed of two ivory tablets depicting Adam and St Paul with identical moulding, as revealed by the borders and by the traces of the hinges which joined them together.

Attribution of the two ivories to the same artist is difficult, since they differ substantially in composition and figure type, although Greek iconography would connect the episode of Adam, who on the sixth day of the Creation named the animals drinking in the four rivers of Paradise, with the miracles of St Paul. The representation of Adam, naked and surrounded by the animals, seems to evoke a pagan bliss allusive to that of Christ (but with the features of Orpheus). The style of the diptych, still classically-influenced, is typical of the years around the late 4th-early 5th century, with a provenance which is not easy to determine (Rome or Byzantium?).

CIRCLE OF CHARLES THE BALD
Tournus Flabellum

Second half 9th century
Bone, ivory, metal and parchment
Height 78 (with fan closed)
Carrand Inv. no. 31

This *flabellum* or fan (flyswatter) bears witness to the secular and liturgical use of a well-documented medieval object (cf. those in the treasuries of Monza and of Canosa). Originating from the abbey of St Philibert of Tournus, it was purchased by Jean-Baptiste Carrand in 1845. Composed of a pleated green-brown-yellowish painted parchment fan, a rectangular case and engraved handle, in the sphere of bas-reliefs and miniatures it is among the masterpieces of ninth-century Carolingian art.

CONSTANTINOPLE
Empress Arianna (?)

Early 6th century
Elephant ivory
30.5×13.6
Carrand Inv. no. 24

This ivory depicting an Empress (Arianna?) once formed the central part of an Imperial polyptych consisting of five tablets. It shows the figure of the empress dressed in a long-sleeved tunic standing on a stool beneath a lavishly decorated dome. Adorned with a heavy necklace and hat, she bears the globe with the cross and sceptre above it (compare with the similar subject in Vienna). The majestic quality of the composition and the prominence of the subject have led to the attribution of the work to the Constantinople area.

MASTER OF THE JUDGEMENT OF PARIS
The Judgement of Paris

c. 1430-1435
Tempera on panel
Diameter 69
Carrand Inv. no. 2026

Executed by an anonymous Florentine painter, this exquisite presentation birth plate with its courtly and profane atmosphere, nevertheless reveals a sensitivity to the influence of Lorenzo Monaco and the forms of Fra Angelico.

The mythological story is divided into three episodes: Paris and his friend the shepherd with his flock of black and white rams, the three goddesses – Venus (with the golden apple of the Hesperides), Juno and Minerva (bearing Eris, the goddess of Discord) –, and in the centre Paris awarding the golden fruit to Aphrodite. The representation, enlivened by an elegant and refined movement, is complemented by the plate in the Le Roy Collection, a replica of the *Carrand Tondo* by the same artist.

MARIANO D'AGNOLO ROMANELLI
Wet-nurse

c. 1390
Polychrome wood
Height 88
Wooden Sculptures Inv. no. 4

This sculpture was purchased in 1904 in Siena by Rudolfo Bassetti. With earlier interpretations including both a *Madonna of the Annunciation* or a *Sibyl*, it presents sufficient evidence for identification as a *Wet-nurse* (the swaddling-roll, the white veil over the hair), a theory which is also confirmed by the squatting pose. It has recently been traced to a Sienese origin, and taken to be the work of Mariano Romanelli.

PARISIAN ART
Standing Madonna with Child

14th century
Ivory
Height 24.4
Ivories Inv. no. 2

This ivory *Madonna with Child*, previously part of the Grand-ducal collection, displays the graceful composition typical of the monumental sculpture produced in France during this period.
Set upon an irregular octagonal pedestal, the figure of the Madonna draped in the sinuous, ample folds of her mantle, with a calm and gentle expression, leans gracefully towards the Child supported by her maternal hand.
The delicate and faintly marked movement of the drapery (simpler and less modulated on the back) and the slenderness of the entire composition enable comparison with contemporary productions of the Paris workshops.

THE TRECENTO ROOM

The connecting room between the Ivories and the Majolica Rooms has been recently reinstalled, housing a selection of sculptures dating from the late 1200s to the 1300s. These works were previously exhibited on the ground floor, which was expanded to accommodate temporary exhibitions. For about twenty years this room housed works now placed throughout the Museum and donated by the Florentine antiquary Giovanni Bruzzichelli. The two large Credenzas *(previously in the Confraternity of the Church of San Michele at Carmignano) and the large* Madonna della Misericordia, *a polychrome wood sculpture from the Tuscan school of the 15th century donated by Luigi Grassi in 1933, remain from the Bruzzichelli installation. The most important pieces, with the highest artistic quality among the marble sculptures, are the* Three Acolytes *(centre of the room) from the workshop of Nicola Pisano, perhaps by Arnolfo di Cambio, and originally one of the pilasters on the* Tomb of St Dominic *in Bologna; the* Child Jesus Blessing, *also attributed to Nicola Pisano's workshop; (against the wall) a* Madonna and Child *and a* Caryatid *(previously part of the sepulchre for Gastone della Torre in the Church of Santa Croce) by Tino di Camaino; an* Angelo with worshiper, *given to Lupo di Francesco. Among the paintings from the 13th and 14th centuries and exhibited here to provide a parallel reference to the sculpture from the same period, there is a thirteenth-century Pisan school* Madonna and Child, *and the* Coronation of the Virgin *by Bernardo Daddi. Recently, an* altarolo *(a small altarpiece) donated in 2000 and depicting the* Madonna and Child with Saints, *work of a follower of Duccio di Boninsegna, has been added to the installation.*

COLLABORATOR OF NICOLA PISANO (ARNOLFO DI CAMBIO?)
Three Acolytes with Censer, Incense-boat, Ampulla

1265-1267

Carrara marble
Height 97 (without base)
Sculpture Inv. no. 409

This sculpture was acquired in 1903 from the Florentine antiquary, Stefano Bardini, who had used it as a base for a flowerpot and then as a support for a holy-water font. It was recognised as one of the supports from the *Tomb of St Dominic* in Bologna and was still in place in 1620. Its Bolognese provenance is confirmed by a sister piece (*Two Acolytes and a Subdeacon*), acquired by the Fine Arts Museum in Boston. Even though various attempts have been made to reconstruct the monument, its original appearance and the exact placement of the small pilasters is unknown. There were various collaborators on the *Tomb of St Dominic*, executed by Giovanni Pisano's workshop. Among these, young Arnolfo di Cambio could have been – along with the help of others – the main contributor on this pilaster. The support function of the three figures, necessarily attached at the central column, has resulted in a handling of the drapery that is flattened, making a stylistic comparison with other works by Arnolfo and other collaborators of Nicola Pisano difficult.

THE MAJOLICA ROOM

The most important (16ᵗʰ century) nucleus of the majolicas on display in this room since 1888 (it previously housed the bronzes) originated in the Urbino workshops, and was built up through gifts and, above all, by the purchases made during the 16ᵗʰ century by the Medici princes. Between the 19ᵗʰ and the 20ᵗʰ centuries it was augmented by the bequests and donations of numerous private citizens (Foresi, Conti, Carrand, Bode, Costantini, Pisa, Vaj Geppi, and recently by Farina Cini, Tesei Manganotti, Bertini, Mazzucconi, the Association of Friends of the Bargello, and Pillitteri). The ware on display (produced by numerous Italian workshops, but also including important examples of Spanish ceramics) illustrates in the variety of shapes and decorations, the different uses to which it was destined. Specific functions included the products for pharmaceutical use such as jars and pots, and tableware such as goblets, plates, water bowls, ewers and mugs. Worthy of note are the items apparently for dining use, but effectively used for the adornment of the sumptuous sideboards in the banqueting-halls: note the Urbino services with historical or grotesque decorations in the two central showcases. On the walls are the large glazed terracotta tondos by Giovanni della Robbia.

FLORENTINE CERAMICS
Zaffera blue relief Jar

Mid 15ᵗʰ century
Glazed terracotta,
initialled with asterisk
under the handles
Height 21.5
Majolica Inv. no. 148

This jar, which came to the Bargello Museum in 1866 with the Conti gift, is decorated with bunches of grapes and oak-leaves in cobalt blue and manganese brown. A typical example of the Florentine ceramic production of the mid-15ᵗʰ century, its shape resembles that of ancient majolica, while the decoration recalls recurrent oriental motifs, and those of Florentine Gothic textile manufacture.

MEDICI PORCELAIN
Basin with St Mark

c. 1580
Porcelain
Diameter 41
Majolica Inv. no. 222

A rare example of Medici porcelain, this basin is decorated with floral motifs, and with St Mark centred on the base (from an engraving by Aldegrever and a design by G. Pencz).
It was made in Florence in the workshops of Francesco I's Casino di San Marco, in imitation of Chinese white and blue porcelain.

URBINO CERAMICS
Water bowl

Second half 16th century
Glazed terracotta
Diameter 51
Majolica Inv. no. 8

Large three-lobed dish depicting Hannibal's encampment (there are three other pieces in the collection). Produced in Urbino (Fontana workshop), it can be recognised among the 'triangular water bowls' decorated "with stories" in Don Antonio's 1588 Medici Inventory. Its shape and ornamental design underline the decorative role it played upon the princely sideboards of the Renaissance.

29

THE LOGGIA (VERONE)

The Verone was constructed by Tone di Giovanni between 1317 and 1320. Francesco Mazzei's nineteenth-century renovation restored the Loggia to its original elegance, re-opening the arches and removing the infrastructure of the prison-cells. During the 19th century it was used to house numerous bells (later transferred to the Museum of San Marco) and various sixteenth-century sculptures, which had come to the Museum from suppressed religious institutions. Several works by Giambologna have been positioned beneath the wide arches: the per-sonifications of Architecture *and* Geometry *(inspired by the* Allegories of the Fine Arts *which in 1564 decorated Michelangelo's funereal catafalque in the Basilica of San Lorenzo) as well as numerous animals in bronze (a* Turkey *from the New World, a* Peacock, *a* Lapwing, *an* Eagle, *an* Eaglet, *a* Rooster, *an* Owl *and* Barn Owls*) made in 1564 for the grotto of the Medici Villa at Castello. Among the reliefs on the walls are* The Drunkenness of Noah *by Baccio Bandinelli*, Diana and Actaeon *by Francesco Moschino (a bas-relief purchased by Cosimo I de' Medici) and various marble medallions which illustrate the classical flavour of the Grand-ducal collections. Acquired in 2001, the monumental statue of* Jason *by Giambologna's student, Pietro Francavilla, has been installed here.*

View of the Loggia (Verone)

PIETRO FRANCAVILLA
Jason

1589
Marble
Height 260
Sculpture Inv. no. 525

The work by Pietro Francavilla, principle assistant along with Pietro Tacca to Giambologna and artist for many works taken from models of the maestro, has been overlooked until recent years, notwithstanding the appreciation expressed by his first biographer, Filippo Baldinucci. The monumental *Jason* is Francavilla's mature masterpiece, signed, and executed in about 1589 for Giovanni Battista Zanchini, an influential figure in Florence at the time. From the centre of the Palazzo Zanchini courtyard in Via Maggio, the mythical argonaut was meant to recall the Medicean undertakings against the Turks carried out by the Order of the Knights of St Stephen to which Zanchini belonged. Francavilla's extraordinary technical ability demonstrated in the monumental nude is particularly well-evidenced by the details, especially the refined carving of the fleece. The artist clearly renders homage to the *Perseus* by Cellini, recognisable in the pose taken by the hero brandishing his trophy. Even though Francavilla's interpretation of the sculpted hero is Late Mannerist, the work descends from Florentine Renaissance sculpture tradition, represented by Michelangelo's *David* and the *St George* by Donatello. When the Zanchini family died out in the 16th century, the *Jason* was passed through heredity ties to the Ricasoli family, who first placed it in the courtyard of their palace in Via Maggio, and then more recently in the palace in Piazza Goldoni. The sculpture was acquired in 2001 by the Italian State for the Bargello Museum.

GIAMBOLOGNA
Owl

1567
Bronze
Height 47
Deposit Inv. no. 2, p. 108

Transferred to the Bargello in 1956, the animals of the Verone illustrate Giambologna's naturalistic intentions. In the *Owl* the natural and hypnotic physicality of the round eyes is highlighted by the geometrical quality of the tufts on the head, while the distended and soft plumage of the body underlines the rigid and balanced posture of this robust bird of prey.

GIAMBOLOGNA
Turkey

1567
Bronze
Height 59
Bronzes Inv. no. 109

The fame of the turkey, imported from America, was consecrated by Giambologna's bronze (while it is also represented in tapestries by Salviati).
The realism of the beak, the neck, the feathers and the wheel of the tail, illustrate in the *Turkey* those same naturalistic intentions of the sculptor, already observed in the *Owl*.

THE DONATELLO HALL

This vast hall, originally designed for the meetings of the Communal Council, after Mazzei's laborious reconstruction was allocated to the exhibition of the monumental sculptures from the Salone dei Cinquecento in the Palazzo Vecchio. It was later planned to transfer the David *from the Piazza della Signoria (now in the Accademia Gallery), so as to reunite it with the other works by Michelangelo already in the Bargello. On the occasion of the Donatello celebrations in 1886, his works from public and private collections, including numerous plaster-casts (among them that of the* Gattamelata*) were gathered together in this spacious room, after which it was decided to allocate the area definitively to the sculpture of the early Florentine Renaissance. As a result of numerous gifts, purchases, and transfers from religious buildings and from the Uffizi Gallery itself, a Donatello Tribuna was set up, displaying his works alongside those of other artists who were active in Florence in the first half of the 15th century (Ghiberti, Brunelleschi, Michelozzo, Luca della Robbia, Agostino di Duccio). The hall is furnished with 14th and 15th century wooden nuptial chests* decorated with paint and pastework, a sacristy *Sideboard, wooden statues including* St Bernardine of Siena *by Vecchietta, and several terracotta* Madonna and Child *(by Antonio di Chellino, by Michelozzo, and by Michele da Firenze).*

DONATELLO
David
[of marble]

1409

Marble
Height 191
Sculpture Inv. no. 2

The marble *David* is the earliest of Donatello's sculptures housed in the Bargello Museum. Sculpted for the apse of Florence Cathedral, in 1416 it was reworked by Donatello himself and transferred to the Palazzo della Signoria as a symbol of Florentine freedom.

One of the sculptor's youthful works, the elegance of the enveloping drapery and the graduated tension of the torso, reveal the rhythms of an influence which is still Gothic-Classical.

DONATELLO
St George
(with detail
of the bas-relief:
*St George liberating
the Princess*)

1416-1417
Marble
Height 209 (statue),
39×120 (bas-relief)
Sculpture Inv. no. 361 (statue),
no. 517 (bas-relief)

Just as in 1402 Brunelleschi's *Abraham's Sacrifice* had marked the start of a new language in bas-relief, so in 1417 – set in the Gothic niche of the Armourers' Guild in the church of Orsanmichele – the *St George* introduced a new concept of perspective.

In his *Lives* (1550) Giorgio Vasari outlined the character of the statue: 'A figure of St George, proud and armed, in whose head we recognise the beauty of his youth, his soul and his valour in arms, a terrible ardour and a marvellous gesture of movement within the stone: it is certain that among modern statues we have not yet seen such animation or feeling in marble as nature and art combine here through the hand of Donato'.

The *St George* blends admirably the medieval significance of hero-saint and the Renaissance sense of individuality. The soul of the statue lies in that powerful movement which Vasari knowledgeably discerns, and which constitutes the foundation of Donatello's art. One or two years later, on the 'pedestal which supports the niche of this, [Donatello] worked a low relief in marble showing the episode of him killing the dragon, with among other things a horse which has been highly valued and praised. In the frontal he carved a half-length figure of God the Father, again in low relief'.

Thus the *St George* marks the beginning of Donatello's two guiding themes: statuary and bas-relief in perspective, where he tackles

the problems of the so-called "flattened relief" in one of its earliest expressions.

After lengthy polemics, the two marbles were brought to the Museum for conservation reasons in 1892, and in 1984 they were replaced on site by copies, and arranged in the Donatello Tribuna of the large first-floor hall.

DONATELLO
Atys

c. 1440

Bronze
(with traces of gilding)
Height 104
Bronzes Inv. no. 448

A work of Donatello's mature period, the *Atys* was bought in 1778 as an antique bronze with gilding, for the Uffizi Gallery from the Doni family for whom it had been made.

Giorgio Vasari in fact recalls in the house of 'Giovambattista d'Agnolo Doni, a Florentine gentleman... a metal Mercury by Donato, three feet high, freestanding, and dressed in a rather bizarre manner, which is truly very beautiful'.
The singularity of the piece has led to the formulation of varying interpretations (Mercury, Atys, a Faun, etc.).

DONATELLO
David [of bronze]
(right)

c. 1440-1450

Bronze; height 158
Bronzes Inv. no. 95

The free-standing life-size bronze *David* reveals in its classically inspired nudity an extraordinary softness of modelling. The sculpture, which is recorded in 1469 in the Medici Palace, was in 1494 taken from the Medici and transferred to the Palazzo Vecchio. From a room in the Pitti Palace to which it had been removed, it subsequently passed to the Uffizi Gallery and thence to the Bargello. Vasari wrote: 'There is, in the courtyard of the Palazzo of these same Signori [Medici] a bronze statue of David, a life-size, nude figure, who having just cut off Goliath's head is raising his foot to place it on him, and he has a sword in his right hand. This figure is so natural in its vivacity and softness, that artists find it hard to believe that it is not moulded over the living form'. The definition of *David* has recently been reinterpreted in a mythological key (*Mercury*), and the dating has been variable (a youthful or mature work).

DONATELLO
Marzocco

1418-1420
Stone with marble inlay
Height 135.5
Sculpture Inv. no. 133

The fame of this sculpture by Donatello, which is ignored by the historical sources, is connected with the nineteenth-century restoration of Palazzo Vecchio and the square outside which had been promoted by the learned historian Giuseppe Del Rosso since 1812. The *Marzocco* (from the

Latin *martius*) the heraldic symbol of Florentine dominion, is represented by a seated lion holding the shield with the lily, the symbol of the Municipality of Florence, under its raised right paw. Sculpted by Donatello between 1418 and 1420 for the apartment of Pope Martin V in Santa Maria Novella, it remained there until 1812, when it was moved to take the place of the considerably damaged fourteenth-century lion in Piazza Signoria. In 1847 it was trans-

ferred to the Uffizi Gallery for conservation reasons (the shield was broken and the back and tail deteriorated), and from there to the Bargello Museum in 1865, where it was displayed at the centre of the Medieval Sculpture Room on the ground floor. The occasion, in 1986, of the sixth Centenary of Donatello's birth promoted its definitive location in the large room dedicated to the Florentine sculptor. The artist has invested the work, a free-standing block of stone, with the same physical and moral power possessed by his *Prophets* on the Campanile. The closed contour defines the massy bulk of the composition, while its vitality is expressed in the rounded back, the leonine stare, the contracted and almost panting jaws, and the realistically reproduced soft, thick waves of the fur. The ornate fifteenth-century base, which bore the Piazza Signoria *Lion* before Donatello's *Marzocco*, has been recently restored and is now rejoined with the *Marzocco* in the centre of the Hall. These original works have been substituted with replicas placed in front of the Palazzo Vecchio.

DONATELLO (?)
Niccolò da Uzzano

c. 1425-1430
Polychrome terracotta
Height 46
Majolica Inv. no. 179

The association of Donatello's name with the terracotta bust of Niccolò da Uzzano from the Capponi residence, appears for the first time in 1745 in Carlo Carlieri's *Florentine Guide*. It was exhibited as a work by Donatello in 1861 at the Guastalla Exhibition, where it attracted purchase negotiations on the part of the Museum of Berlin. In 1881 it was purchased by the Italian State exercising the rights of pre-emption, and assigned to the Bargello collections. Of all illustrious Florentines, Niccolò da Uzzano (a prestigious public figure, responsible for the creation of the Studio Fiorentino) enjoyed an exceptional degree of visual documentation, with his image appearing on numerous frescoes, medals and prints of the period. His portrait can still be seen in Benozzo Gozzoli's *Procession of the Magi* (1459-1464) in the Palazzo Medici-Riccardi, in the choir of the Church of Santa Lucia de' Magnoli and in the Uffizi Gallery itself (in the vaults and in a copy of the Giovio Series of famous men). Iconographic doubts (another bust portraying Bernardo da Uzzano has been lost, and the theory proposed that this might be a representation of Cicero or Pier Capponi), as well as doubts about Donatello's authorship have been expressed since the 19th century. Following a restoration carried out by the Opificio delle Pietre Dure in 1986, the work has nevertheless been subject to reappraisal. The restoration of the bust to the classical harmony of its original vertical position and the removal of the superficial layer of paint, have brought to light an extraordinary plastic and chromatic surface (observe the superbly expressive treatment of the transition from the skin to the unshaved stubble of the beard) such as to effectively suggest an attribution to Desiderio da Settignano if not to Donatello himself.

LORENZO GHIBERTI
Abraham's Sacrifice
(Relief panel
from the Baptistry)
1402
Gilded bronze
44×40
Bronzes Inv. no. 203

In 1402 Lorenzo Ghiberti created the panel with 'Abraham sacrificing his son Isaac' for the competition for the second door of the Baptistery of Florence (the first was created by Andrea Pisano). Vasari wrote that the competitors were 'Filippo Brunelleschi, Donatello and Lorenzo di Bartoluccio (all Florentines) and Jacopo della Quercia of Siena, Niccolò Aretino, his pupil, Francesco di Valdambrina and Simone dal Colle'.

Ghiberti was the winner: his work was 'excellently composed: the figures, showing the individuality of his style, were lively, gracefully wrought with lovely expressions and the whole finished with such diligence that it seemed not to have been cast and reworked with irons, but rather forged by pure breath'.

Included in the Medici Guardaroba in 1587, the panel passed to the Bargello in 1865.

FILIPPO BRUNELLESCHI
Abraham's Sacrifice
(Relief panel
from the Baptistry)
1402
Gilded bronze
47×40
Bronzes Inv. no. 209

Although on the same theme, Filippo Brunelleschi's panel is very different. Lorenzo Ghiberti's rich decorative sensitivity and exquisite technique is countered by Brunelleschi's incisive movement, which with its echoes of a still-Gothic drapery, presents an action made up of rapid and dramatic gestures. The story 'which he had worked in bronze' was then donated to Cosimo de' Medici for the altar frontal of the Old Sacristy of San Lorenzo in Florence.
Under Pietro Leopoldo, it passed to the Uffizi, and later transferred to the Bargello in 1865, together with the other bronzes held in the Gallery. In the present layout the two panels are displayed quite close to each other on the same wall, enabling a comparison of Ghiberti's still archaic models with the innovative figurative and spatial language of Filippo Brunelleschi.

THE ISLAMIC ROOM

This room is devoted to the exhibition of the works of Islamic art which came to the Bargello from the ancient Grand-ducal collections, and to a greater extent through the Carrand, Ressman and Franchetti collections. In the eighteen-eighties it housed the Zumbo waxworks from the Museum of the Specola, and later the Museum's collection of medieval seals along with the Carrand tapestries. Currently on display are examples of superior-level Islamic metalwork in bronze, silver and brass, with exceptionally intricate decorative finishes, some of them engraved, as illustrated by two Incense-burners *(Syria, 14th-15th century), a* Vase *(Persia, 15th century) and a hemispheric* Box *with cover, signed Zain ad-Din (15th century, Venetian-Saracen art), exhibited from 1587 in the Tribuna of the Uffizi Gallery.*

Also particularly worthy of note are several works of art of the Venetian-Saracen school, i.e. produced by oriental artists active in Venice, such as Trays *and* Boxes, *a small bronze* Mirror, *a* Bowl *and a* Goblet *engraved and encrusted with gold and silver, made in Cairo for a Yemen sultan in the Mameluke period (between 1363 and 1377). Of exceptional importance are the ivories (see the* Horn, *and the* Elephant *chess-piece made in Mesopotamia in the 9th century), the Persian and Turkish arms (15th, 16th and 17th centuries), the glass* Mosque-lamp *commissioned and donated to the place of worship by the Emir as-Sayfi Tughaytamur an-Nasiri (as shown by the painted inscription), the* Holbein *and* Lotto *carpets, so-called after the artists who have depicted them in their paintings, and the textile exhibits, which for conservation reasons are shown in rotation. Among the ceramics worthy of note are the splendid multicoloured Persian and Turkish "metallic lustre"* Tiles, *and two* Turkish plates *(Iznik ceramics), the rarer of the two donated in 2002.*

SYRIA
Spherical two-part incense-burner

14th century

Brass, damascened silver
Diameter 11
Bronzes Inv. no. 299

This incense-burner is recorded in the Medici collections of 1587, and later in the famous "cabinet" of the same room. It is decorated with rosettes, palm-leaves and circular bands in beaten brass, pierced and damascened in silver.

EGYPT
Six plaquettes with hunting and court scenes

9th-12th centuries

Ivory sculpted and engraved
17×7.5 and 6.3×12.2
Carrand Inv. no. 80

The Bargello Islamic ivories, datable between the 9th and 12th centuries, of a Spanish or Southern cultural origin, are of an exceptional artistic quality.
The six plaquettes, which may have formed part of the same object

(casket, door?) come, like most of the ivories, from the Carrand Collection. Produced in Egypt during the Fatimid period (909-1171) they reveal an extraordinary engraving technique in representations of the hunt and the court.
Particularly striking are the drapery of the garments, the mimicry of the faces and the delicacy of the "lace" effects of the floral decorations.

KASHAN (PERSIA)
Tile

13th-14th centuries
Metallic lustre ceramic
31.5×26
Carrand Inv. no. 1970

The Bargello's collection of oriental majolica is largely composed of metallic lustre wall tiles. The exemplar shown here is in the form of a five-pointed star with one straight side, decorated with an abstract floral design with an Italic inscription from the Koran. Tiles similar to this one, which are considered to originate from the Iraqi mausoleum of Yahya di Varamin, are conserved in the Victoria and Albert Museum in London.

SYRIA
Mosque Lamp
(below)

1342-1345
Blown glass, enamel
Height 35.8
Carrand Inv. no. 2005

Mosque lamps, similar to the exemplar shown here, were produced in the workshops of the craftsman glaziers of Damascus and Aleppo from the 12th century on. These coloured and painted elegantly-shaped glasses (usually designed for lamps formed of two truncated cones with a tall, wide flared neck) were ordered by sultans and Mameluke dignitaries to adorn the Mosques.

The painted inscription and the coats-of-arms stamped on the medallions bear the name of the Emir who, in the mid 14th century ordered the Bargello Museum *Mosque Lamp*.

THE CARRAND ROOM

This room, which was previously dedicated to the Duke of Athens on account of the recurrent representation of his coat-of-arms, has since 1888 housed the most prestigious examples of Gothic and Renaissance "minor arts" left to the Bargello in his will by the French collector Louis Carrand. The works on exhibit are subdivided by type and reveal the eclectic tastes of the nineteenth-century collector. Among the most representative pieces are the ancient and modern Jewellery, *the numerous* Limoges enamels, *the shell* Cameos, *the Flemish and French* Metalwork, *the* Cutlery, *the* Surgical Instruments, *the* Objects in Iron, *the interesting selection of* Buckles, *the rare examples of* Indian Art, *and the typical "Wunderkammer" pieces. On the walls, alongside the small gold ground panel paintings is the famous* Carrand Diptych *from the fourteenth-century Parisian school, and wooden sculptures of the* Angel *and the* Virgin Annunciate *of the Sienese school.* Glass objects *with various origins dating from the 16th to 18th centuries have recently been put on display, along with a rare* Sorrowing Virgin *in polychrome wood by a Florentine mannerist sculptor (c. 1525), accessioned in 2001.*

LIMOGES
Plaque

c. 1180
Gilded copper, engraved
champlevé enamel
24.9×9.3
Carrand Inv. no. 632

The parable of the wise and foolish virgins from *St Matthew's Gospel*, which was so widely illustrated in Palaeo-Christian art and later in Romanesque and Gothic sculpture and miniatures, also appears in the Limoges enamel artefacts. An example is provided by this synthetic image of the *Wise Virgin* – part of a series of ten plaques destined for the decoration of the frontal or ancon of an altar – characterised by the deep lines and marked by an all-enveloping linear rhythm. The head in relief has enamelled eyes.

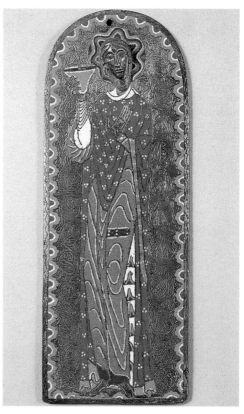

BYZANTIUM
Earrings

5th-9th centuries
Bronze, silver; diameter c. 4
Secular Jewellery Inv.
nos. 102, 107

The two table showcases in this room contain numerous examples of secular jewellery, the Byzantine and Frankish nucleus of which was almost entirely gathered by Louis Carrand. Earrings, pendants, brooches and rings came to form a small collection which is of considerable significance in terms of the sumptuous late-Roman and Byzantine jewellery manufacture. In 1985 the Carrand nucleus was augmented by other exemplars, thanks to the generosity of Enrico d'Assia who donated a large number of earrings so that the Bargello Museum might possess the entire range of the various Byzantine types covering the period from the 5th to the 9th century.

LONGOBARD ART
Agylulf's plate

6th-7th centuries
Gilded copper
18.9×6.7
Bronzes Inv. no. 681

The famous *Agylulf's Plate*, in engraved relief-work, was discovered in 1891 in Valdinievole (Lucca). The trapezoidal plate has been variously interpreted as the ornamental decoration of a helmet, or of a throne or chair. It portrays Agylulf (King of the Longobards or Lombards from 591 to 615-616) as confirmed by the punched inscription "Dn Agilulf regi", who by his sword and raised right hand reveals his regal powers: to command and to judge. Late antique influences (diptychs, Byzantine and Longobard coins) as well as Christian models (mosaics and sarcophagi) are blended with ingenuous expressivity in the faces and clothing of the various figures.

GERMANY
Acquamanile
(with detail)

c. 1400

Bronze
41×36.2
Carrand Inv. no. 330

Displayed alongside two other older Acquamanili also from the Carrand Collection, this exemplar is striking for its "shiny" bronze finish and for its refined modelling. Particularly noteworthy is the fine engraving of the horse's caparison and harness, as well as the grace and vivacity of the entire equestrian composition. Although designed for use with a dinner service, the figure of the famous *Acquamanile*, previously interpreted as *St George*, reveals in his military dress a blending of German and French elements typical of the early 15th century.

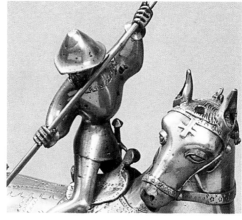

CONQUES
Medallion

12th century

Gilded copper,
champlevé enamel
Diameter 10
Carrand Inv. no. 625

The four Carrand medallions (only six others, slightly different, are known) during the 19th century were believed to be decorations from a military belt. In the light of more recent studies, they are now considered to be the ornaments from a casket similar to that preserved at the Abbey of Conques. The green, azure and white decorations, highlighted by a border with a geometrical "Z" design, show real and fantastic animals which are related to the ancient oriental textile repertory of griffons and winged lions. On the back the four plaques show traces of a fastening.

FRANCE OR FLANDERS
Bag

16th century

Embroidered leather,
burnished and gilded metal
28×26
Carrand Inv. no. 1810

The bags made of various materials typical of the period between the 14th and the 16th centuries, with illustrations of court life, were particularly popular among nineteenth-century collectors. This example is made of a central section closed by an iron hoop, with six smaller pockets embellished with lace trimmings and embroidery.

BURGUNDY
*Married couple
in profile*

15th-16th centuries
(frame 17th century)

Shell cameo
with gold frame
6.5×5.3 (frame 1.3)
Carrand Inv. no. 1291

The fine and compact granular structure of the shell has enabled the creation of this extraordinary finely-carved specimen. The theory that the cameo, with its charming representation of a couple in affectionate embrace, was made in France, is confirmed by the French inventory documentation of numerous objects made of shell.

BENVENUTO CELLINI
*Hatpin with
"Leda and the Swan"*

c. 1528-1530

Gold, lapis lazuli,
enamel, pearls
Diameter 5.8
Deposit Inv. no. 1, p. 16

This superb *Hatpin* decorated with a representation of *Leda and the Swan*, previously in the Strozzi Sacrati Collection in Florence, was deposited in the Museum in recent years by the Soprintendenza of Bologna. The materials used – gold, pearls, lapis lazuli and enamel – and their skilful and exqui- site combination recall Michelangelo's analogous composition, while the workmanship re- flects and is mirrored by that of Benvenuto Cellini's *Salt-cellar*, now in Vienna.

BRUSSELS (?)
Goblet

Second half 16th century
Coconut, silver
and gilded copper
Height 35.5
Carrand Inv. no. 788

An example of an object typical of the "Wunderkammer", or collection of marvels, which enjoyed such great popularity in Europe in the second half of the 16th century. Feathers, minerals, ostrich eggs and cuttlebone were combined into the most bizarre and fantastic shapes, frequently designed by famous artists and sculptors. Here the erotic subjects represented on the ovoid part of the coconut suggest that this was probably a "lovers' cup".

FRANCE
Cosmometer
16th century

Wood, paper, brass; 36.1×32.9
Carrand Inv. no. 1171

This instrument, unique of its kind, is associated with the study of the Earth in relation to geophysical observations and calculations and topographical measurement. It is composed of a double-sided plank of wood covered with painted paper and bordered with brass. *Music* and *Astrology* are represented on the front, beneath the circle of latitude and longitude. It was designed in Paris by Jacques Chauvet in 1585.

FRANCE
*Diptych with
Sacra Conversazione
and Crucifixion*

Late 14th century

Oil on panel
90×29
Carrand Inv. no. 2062

Like the frame for a precious missal or a jewel, the setting of these two sacred-courtly pictures is made up of an elaborate mixture of architectural features (pinnacles, flying buttresses and balusters) suggesting the doorway of a Gothic cathedral, highlighted on the inner borders by gold, rosettes and red and blue semiprecious stones.

The "large" *Carrand Diptych*, so-called to distinguish it from another diptych in the Collection known as "small" is a masterpiece of the collection even as an individual work of art.

Since its arrival in the Museum in 1888 it has attracted the attention of scholars, who have attributed it to various schools and dates – Burgundy, Paris, Avignon, Flanders – up to the mature period of Michelino da Besozzo, or to a collaborator of Jean de Berry.

The identification of the betrothed couple in the left-hand scene as Catherine, daughter of Charles V, and Count John of Montpensier, son of Jean de Berry, portrayed in ceremonial armour, whom she married in 1386, has led to the location of the painting in France (in the Duke de Berry's miniature workshop), and to a dating which corresponds with that of Catherine's marriage.

The emblem of the French house is clearly indicated by the allusive white lily held delicately aloft in Catherine's slender fingers. In its celebration of the event the princely commission of the *Diptych* is implicit, while in its late-Gothic-courtly refinement it participates, through the figure of the Virgin-mother, in the mystery of the birth and death of Christ.

THE MAGDALENE'S CHAPEL

The Bargello Chapel, which in the eighteen-forties was divided into two floors for use respectively as storeroom and prison quarters, played a crucial role in the history of the Palazzo and the future Museum. Contemporary historical studies, referring to popular memory (confirmed by Vasari), indicated the chapel as the site of frescoes by Giotto (attributed to Giotto's workshop) and of the portrait of Dante, 'his contemporary and great friend' portrayed together with 'Sir Brunetto Latini ... and milord Corso Donati'. The suggestion on the part of foreign personages to restore the building did not convince Paolo Feroni, the future Director of the Uffizi Gallery, who commissioned a series of tests and later instigated the restoration through the Lorraine administration (restorer, Antonio Marini). The discovery of the portrait of Dante on 20 July 1840 led to the circulation of the image of the divine poet and of the Chapel itself through the press, which contributed to the request for the restoration of the entire complex from a variety of quarters. The evocative furnishings, composed of the wooden Choir Stalls *and the high* Lectern *in the centre (both from the Abbey of Monteoliveto) have been further enhanced by numerous sacred (in the showcase to the right on entering) and ecclesiastical ornaments (in that to the left) originating from the Carrand Collection. The* Triptych *by Giovanni di Francesco embellished by Andrea di Puccio's* Altar-step, *previously in the Florence Baptistry, alludes to the altar in the area of the bottom niche.*

GIOVANNI DI FRANCESCO known as **CERVELLIERA**
Triptych with Madonna, Child and Saints

c. 1450
Tempera on panel
182×165
Carrand Inv. no. 2025

The stylistic comparison with the *God the Father in Benediction* in the entrance lunette of the Church of the Innocenti has connected this *Triptych* – which at the end of the 19th century was attributed to the "Master of the Carrand Triptych" and the artist known as "Pesello" – with Giovanni di Francesco, a pupil of Andrea del Castagno, who in 1442 was registered in the Guild of Doctors and Chemists. The altarpiece represents the *Madonna and Child with Sts Francis, John the Baptist, Nicholas and Peter* and, in the upper border the *Annunciation*, the *Incoronation of Our Lady* and the *Assumption*.

It originally belonged to the Gianni Chapel of the Church of San Niccolò in "Oltrarno". Here the perspective and the decorum of the images blend and combine typical elements of late fifteenth-century Florentine painting, as illustrated by Filippo Lippi, Andrea del Castagno, Paolo Uccello and Domenico Veneziano.

In view of the small number of known and dated works by this artist (other than the *God the Father in Benediction*, there is the *San Biagio* of the Church at Petriolo) the Bargello *Triptych* has been approximately - dated around the mid-15th century.

THE SACRISTY

The recent reorganisation of the Museum, along with related research, has resulted in a desire to create an equilibrium between the monumental Palazzo and its collections. The Magdalene's Chapel and the adjacent Sacristy suggested the ideal setting for the Bargello's sacred objects in gold. Consequently this area, limited in space but with an admirable architectural structure, was laid out for the display of these precious objects in showcases recalling the cupboards of the ancient sacristies. Among the most important pieces (once ecclesiastical ornaments and illustrative of liturgical use) are Antonio del Pollaiolo's Crucifix *with its translucent enamels, the slightly earlier series of* Paxes *with their exquisite niello work, the processional and altar* Crosses *from the 13th and 14th centuries, and the gilded bronze* Tondo, *attributed to Luca della Robbia (previously in the Tabernacle of Santa Maria a Peretola). Also remarkable is the large* Abyssinian Cross *from the second half of the 15th century originally in the Grand-ducal collections as well as the small altar with the* Flagellation *attributed to Guglielmo della Porta, the later* Christ at the Pillar *and the three* Pastoral Staves *from Florentine and Lombard schools of the 15th, 16th and 17th centuries.*

PARIS
Pax with St John the Baptist

15th century
Gold, gilded silver, enamel, pearls and rubies
Height 13.3
Sacred Jewellery Inv. no. 39

This jewel, originally the central section of a tabernacle (mentioned in the Inventories of Jean de Berry, 1402), acquired the liturgical function of a pax after a nineteenth-century restoration during which the saint's halo, the base and the frame were reconstructed. It portrays St John the Baptist with the Lamb in the centre against a background of red brocade cloth borne up by angels. The elegance of the piece is highlighted by enamels and precious stones.

WORKSHOP OF
ANTONIO SALVI
Pax with Deposition

c. 1480-1490

Silver, enamel
with inscription
on the frieze
21.4×14.5
Sacred jewellery Inv. no. 38

This *Pax* is shaped like
an arched tabernacle
with a structure in silver
comprising an architec-
tural frame with two an-
gels in relief and a series
of illustrated enamelled
plaquettes. In the back-
ground is the *Lamenta-
tion of Christ* with the
prophets *Isaiah* and *Je-
remiah* (below) and *God
the Father with cherubs*
(above). The decorated
and engraved back re-
veals a very distinctive
circlet handle.

ANTONIO POLLAIOLO
and **UNKNOWN**
GOLDSMITH
Reliquary Cross

1476-1483 (enamels)
1500-1530 (Cross)

Silver, enamel,
gilded bronze, wood
57×48
Sacred Jewellery Inv. no. 15

This *Cross* was made for
the Monastery of San
Gaggio, and may have
been cast on the occa-
sion of the Florentine
siege of 1530. The six
plaquettes which were
later remounted, came
to the Bargello in 1865.

55

THE GIOVANNI DELLA ROBBIA ROOM

Returning to the Ivories Room we ascend to the second floor to reach the room which in 1884 housed the series of frescoes of Famous Men and Women by Andrea del Castagno, previously in the Villa of Legnaia and now at San Pier Scheraggio. This room now contains glazed terracottas by Giovanni della Robbia, and by the Buglioni family, and the later production of their workshops. The "robbias", mostly destined for places of worship between the end of the 15th century and the first half of the 16th, bear witness to a flourishing craft activity which continued to respect the earlier inventions of Luca della Robbia. The creations of Giovanni, son of Andrea, are distinguished by the use of polychrome glazes, the narrative variety of the subjects, and the richness of details and decorations. Compare the youthful Adoration of the Magi *with the* Pietà *of Via della Scala and the famous* Crib *of the early decades of the 16th century, which came to the Bargello in 1865 from the suppressed Convent of San Girolamo delle Poverine. In the same years Giovanni's activity came to measure itself against that of the Buglioni workshop. (See the* Madonna and Child *by Benedetto Buglioni with its bright transparent colours, derived from a composition by Antonio Rossellino, and the* Noli me tangere *by Benedetto and Santi Buglioni of the Convent of Sant'Orsola). The room also houses the monumental* Lament *in terracotta, at one time glazed in polychrome, believed to be by Andrea della Robbia (c. 1510) and accessioned in 1998. Also on display are works by Giovan Francesco Rustici and Sansovino. In the centre is a collection of Renaissance plaquettes, most of which belonged to the Medici Grand Dukes.*

**GIOVANNI
DELLA ROBBIA**
Pietà

1514
Glazed terracotta
300×228
Robbie Inv. no. 64

The large arched ancon of the *Pietà with St John and Mary Magdalene grieving*, created in 1514 for the Cappella dell'Orto of the Hospital of Santa Maria della Scala, reveals a lively polychromatic use of the figures, backgrounds, and of the fantastic decorative designs. The centre of the predella, with a devout but mannered *Annunciation*, is balanced by the crowded row of putti in swaddling clothes and the coats-of-arms of Cardinal Accolti and of the Pollini family.

THE ANDREA DELLA ROBBIA ROOM

This room is dedicated to the "inventions" of Andrea della Robbia who, in his large, well-organised Via Guelfa workshop, skilfully exploited the glazing technique to its utmost. The rich Robbia production of devout images for domestic use, as well as large-scale altarpieces, found an extensive market. Andrea was acquainted with the architects of his time, with the painters, among them Benozzo Gozzoli, Ghirlandaio, Filippino Lippi, Fra Bartolomeo, and with the sculptors. This fact, along with the commissions both from illustrious private individuals (such as members of the Medici circle) and from religious bodies (the Franciscan and Dominican orders) led to the works of Andrea della Robbia reaching a large number of courts and churches throughout Europe. The descriptive pictorial tones of his youthful Madonnas, which were frequently reproduced in the same workshop by his numerous collaborators, developed into a serene and tender portrayal which was sensitive to the tendencies of the time. Observe the Madonna of the Architects *(1475), the* Madonna of the Cushion *from the suppressed Convent of the Church of the Badia, or the tondo of the* Madonna and Child*. To the right on the wall, we find the famous medallion with a* Portrait of a Young Girl *and the tender bust,* Portrait of a Boy*, both with a sensitively natural modelling and a refined chromatic range in the glazes. Between the two windows there is a stone* Lavabo *with the Acciaioli-Federighi crests dating to about 1499, part of the Museum since 1866. The display cases contain a selection of an exceptional collection of civil and religious seals, and a sampling of coins from Florence (13ᵗʰ-18ᵗʰ centuries) and Tuscany (13ᵗʰ-16ᵗʰ centuries).*

ANDREA DELLA ROBBIA
*Portrait
of a Young Girl*

c. 1475

Glazed terracotta
Diameter 37
Robbie Inv. no. 73

This delicate medallion-shaped *Portrait of a Young Girl* came to the Bargello in 1879 from the Uffizi Gallery. The long, slender neck, the hairstyle, and the precious and elegant jewellery, suggest, through an atmospheric depth of intense azure, the idealised portrait of a Florentine noblewoman.

ANDREA DELLA ROBBIA
Portrait of a Boy

c. 1474

Glazed terracotta
Height 37
Robbie Inv. no. 75

This bust came to the Bargello Museum in 1902 from the Hospital of Santa Maria Nuova, and is possibly a portrait of Peter the Unfortunate, son of Lorenzo the Magnificent. Its tender and youthful contours, and the intimacy of the expression, indicate both the *pathos* and vitality of the child portrayed.

ANDREA DELLA ROBBIA
The Madonna of the Architects

1475

Glazed terracotta
135×96
Robbie Inv. no. 74

The *Madonna of the Architects* is the earliest recorded work by Andrea, commissioned from him in 1475 by the Guild of the Master Stone and Woodworkers.
The superbly gentle and tender effects of form blend with the graceful heads of the cherubs and the elegant frame (which bears the name of the Guild in the lower section on a porphyry-red ground).

THE BRONZES ROOM

This room houses one of the most numerous of the Museum's collections: bronzes of varied provenance. They include those of Medici origin, which were exhibited throughout the 18th century in the Uffizi Gallery, those from the Palazzo Vecchio, the Palazzo Pitti and the Villa of Poggio Imperiale, as well as the nucleus bequeathed to the Bargello in 1888 by Louis Carrand. The popularity of the bronze statuettes – which range from mythological interpretation to antique inspiration and from the generic to the useful (mortars, lamps, bells, animals) – is connected with the collection of pieces from the sixteenth-century workshops or of "Wunderkammer" on the part of the aristocratic courts. In Florence the refined taste of Lorenzo the Magnificent had, through Donatello, Bertoldo and Pollaiolo, anticipated this blending of artistic ingenuity with an extraordinary casting technique. These small bronzes, which were originally displayed together with the large bronzes in the first-floor room, were transferred after the Second World War into what is now the Armoury, and finally found their definitive home in the present room.

GIAMBOLOGNA
Kneeling nymph surprised while bathing

c. 1560
Bronze; height 9.7
Bronzes Inv. no. 69

60

collection of this famous and refined genre.

This bronze, which is almost a companion-piece to the *Young woman kneeling, drying herself*, derives from the classic style of the *Venere* of Doidalsas in Rome, at the time of the artist's second visit.

The restlessness typical of the large and complex naturalistic compositions of the School of Fontainebleau, is translated in the small plastic forms of Giambologna into an abstract, poised elegance balanced by spiral rhythms, and enriched through subtle variations.

This small sculpture is located in space by the multiplication of viewing angles, in a vision which is the opposite of that of Michelangelo Buonarroti.

The conspicuous number of Grand-ducal bronzes in the Bargello which are attributed to Giambologna testifies to the Medici passion for the

ANTONIO POLLAIOLO
Hercules and Antaeus

c. 1478

Bronze; height 45
Bronzes Inv. no. 280

The incisive and sinewy contours of this bronze recall what Vasari wrote in his *Lives*: 'He understood the nude in a more modern sense than other masters before him, and he dissected many bodies to observe their underlying anatomy'. Along with the *Labours of Hercules*, painted several years earlier for the Medici in the Via Larga Palace, the inventory made on the death of Lorenzo the Magnificent recorded 'A Hercules combating Antaeus, all in bronze, 1/3 braccia tall'. The intense expressive quality is naturalistically rendered by the strained muscles and by the dramatic tension on the faces of the two clenched figures.

61

GIAMBOLOGNA
and **VINCENZO
DELLA NERA**
Morgante the Dwarf

1582-1583

Bronze (the marble base
is modern); width 36.5
Bronzes Inv. no. 9

Morgante was the court
dwarf from the time of
Cosimo I to that of Fer-
dinand I; the bronze is a
work of collaboration between Giambologna who
created the figure of the
dwarf and the goldsmith
Vincenzo della Nera (for
the dragon). It was com-
missioned by Francesco
I de' Medici as an elegant
crowning ornament for
the fountain of the hang-
ing garden above the
Loggia dei Lanzi.

ANDREA BRIOSCO
known as **IL RICCIO**
Goat

Second half of 16th century

Bronze
(base in wood)
18×19×4
Bronzes Inv. no. 380

The popularity of small
bronzes during the Re-
naissance was not limi-
ted to the circle of the
Medici court, but exten-
ded to many other cen-
tres of Northern Italy,
such as Venice, Mantua
and Padua (where the
presence of Donatello
was a determining fac-
tor). The Venetian ex-
amples are particularly
well-represented in the
Bargello Museum, with
works by Riccio, San-
sovino and their collab-
orators. Pieces by Riccio
include *Jupiter and the
goat Amaltea*, the *Triton*,
the *Satyr with vase and
shell* and the *Goat*, with
its naturally delineated
muzzle and shaggy, curly
coat. Present in the Medici Casino of San Marco
from 1588, the bronze is
mounted on an oval base
of pale walnut with stone
decorations like those
described in the inven-
tories of the period.

THE VERROCCHIO ROOM

From 1873 on this room has been used for the display of Tuscan sculpture from the second half of the 15th century, much of which has come from the Uffizi Gallery, with Medici works and purchases made during the first half of the 19th century. Hanging on the walls and on high stools engraved and highlighted in gold, are the portraits of numerous historical figures, among them the merchant Piero Mellini *by Benedetto da Maiano (signed and dated 1474), the Florentine historian* Matteo Palmieri *(signed and dated 1478) and* Francesco Sassetti *(both by Antonio Rossellino),* Piero de' Medici, *the noble* Rinaldo della Luna *(signed and dated 1461),* Giovanni de' Medici *(all three by Mino da Fiesole) and the* Noblewoman with Bouquet *(previously attributed to Donatello himself) and* Battista Sforza, *wife of Federico da Montefeltro (painted by Francesco Laurana, which came to Florence from Urbino with the inheritance of Vittoria della Rovere, bride of Ferdinando de' Medici). Nevertheless, the best-represented artist is Andrea Verrocchio 'Florentine... and in his time, goldsmith, master of perspective, sculptor, engraver, painter and musician'. The decoration of the room is completed by a large* Sacristy sideboard *from the end of the 15th century, and numerous neo-Renaissance* Chests.

ANDREA VERROCCHIO, *Resurrection*

ANDREA VERROCCHIO
David
(with details)

c. 1465

Bronze, partially gilded
Height 120
Bronzes Inv. nos. 450, 451

With its very obvious historic-symbolic significance in the sphere of civic liberty, Verrocchio's *David*, property of the Medici family, was purchased in 1476 by the Florentine Signoria for Palazzo Vecchio. Placed on the landing outside the Sala dei Gigli, and near the Porta della Catena, the *David* was a very precise reference to the procedures in the Florentine government. The studies made on the work during its restoration revealed that it was transferred to a column with a surface smaller than its original base, thus necessitating a change in the placement of Goliath's head to between David's legs. During the 17th century the *David* was moved to the Uffizi where it was separated from the head of Goliath. In this way it lost both its Biblical significance and also the name of its creator, remaining catalogued under the title of "Youthful Mars", being neglected until the late 19th century. In about 1870 it was transferred to the Bargello. The commission was destined for a secular domestic ambience, confirmation of which is found in the rich gilding, uncovered during the recent restoration, on the hair, the breastplate and boots. The *David* anticipated Verrocchio's full potential as a sculptor, which was to be confirmed in the *Christ and St Thomas* (1466). The classical references, the intense vitality of the light in the facial transitions, combined with an exceptional technical perfection, establish the Bargello's Biblical hero as one of the masterpieces of the Italian Renaissance.

ANDREA VERROCCHIO
*Noblewoman
with Bouquet*
(with details)

1475-1480
Marble
Height 57
Sculpture Inv. no. 115

This work came to the Bargello from the Uffizi Gallery where it was preserved as a masterpiece by Donatello. This rather secluded history of the piece has rendered difficult the identification of the subject. This noblewoman with a bou-

quet has been variously recognised as Ginevra de' Benci (because of the similarity with Leonardo's famous portrait in the Washington National Gallery) and Lucrezia Donati (platonically beloved of Lorenzo the Magnificent, and whose

effigy was recorded in Lorenzo's chamber in 1492). The symbolic interpretation of the bouquet (primroses, but also wild roses or hibiscus), if it were resolved, could assist the deciphering of the portrait. Classic in its front-facing pose, yet disturbingly innovative in the hairstyle, the spontaneity of gesture, and the radiant smoothness of the skin, the superb quality of the work identifies it within Verrocchio's stylistic development, and it has been assigned by the critics to the artist's mature period. In the richly evocative poise of the gathered hands, at once vital and delicate, some have recognised the touch of the young Leonardo, who was an apprentice in Verrocchio's workshop during this period.

ANDREA VERROCCHIO
Crucifix
(detail)

c. 1480
Polychrome wood
Height 103
Deposit Inv. no. 1, p. 91

The *Crucifix* which came to the Bargello in 1994 from the Florentine Confraternity of St Francis in Piazza della Santissima Annunziata, is the only known example of the "wooden crucifixes" made by Verrocchio and recorded by Vasari. A distinctive chromatic softness lends the sculpture a disturbing *pathos*, and an intense and felt emotive sensibility which is characteristic of the artist's finest work; it provides an exceptional illustration of the direct relationship between plastic and pictorial language, or rather the combination and subtle blending of the two.

The Baroque Sculpture and Medals Rooms

These two rooms are now dedicated to the display of the Bargello's Baroque sculpture and the most prestigious medals from the Medagliere Mediceo. Like the rest of the Museum, this area was included in Mazzei's 1860 restoration, and in 1897, after the transfer of the Medici Medals collection from the Uffizi Gallery, was given over entirely to these exhibits. After the theft of a medal by Pisanello they were closed and excluded from the Museum circuit. This genre of microsculpture, which enjoyed such popularity in the history of the Medici collections (the medal as portrait, and as symbol and celebration of specific events) has been reappraised in recent years, and the collection has been augmented by the planned purchases made betwin 1980 and 1997. As a result the Grand-ducal Medagliere, completely reorganised in chronological order, is now exhibited alongside the examples of Baroque sculpture. At the centre of the first room is the Bust of Costanza Bonarelli, *accompanied by the monumental* Cardinal Rondanini, *as well as by Massimiliano Soldani's exuberant and refined bas-reliefs and by Poggini's* Nova Lex *itself in the second room. Recently installed are a* Bust of Christ *by Tullio Lombardo, acquired in 2001, and some refined Classical-style marble reliefs, four of which are from the circle of Antonio Lombardo and are related to the decorations in Alfonso d'Este's "alabaster rooms" in Ferrara.*

Gian Lorenzo
Bernini

Bust of Costanza Bonarelli

1636
Marble
Height 69
Sculpture Inv. no. 81

This bust came from the Uffizi Gallery, where it was exhibited from 1645 in the First corridor next to Michelangelo Buonarroti's *Brutus*.
The figure, redolent of Rubenesque influences, emerges marvellously balanced in the play of the slightly disordered garments and the hair, in the sensual rounded contours of the flesh and the robust neck.

ALESSANDRO ALGARDI
Bust of Cardinal
Paolo Emilio Zacchia
Rondanini

c. 1650

Marble
Height 100
Sculpture Inv. no. 512

The cardinal, whose bust rests on a section of pillar in variegated marble, is turning over with his left hand the pages of a book held in his right. Giovan Battista Bellori includes the sculpture in a generic reference made in his *Lives of the Painters*: '...most beautiful are the Cardinal Antonio of Santa Croce and the Cardinal Zacchia Rondanini, this latter in the act of turning the page of a book which he is

holding in his hands'. It originally belonged to the Rondanini family, and later formed part of the Ojetti collection in Florence. In 1983 it was purchased by the Italian State for the Bargello Museum Baroque collection.

On Algardi's death, it was listed among the artist's unfinished works, and later modifications cannot be excluded given the absence of documentary evidence.

Throughout his career the artist conceived the half-figure as a monumental genre. The expressive intensity of the face, the sensitivity of the tapered fingers and the fine pleating of the tunic which is revealed under the cape, make this an exemplar of an exceptional level.

These qualities, which mark the point of closest resemblance to Bernini, might have been more marked had the work been terminated and the finishing touches given by Algardi himself. A terracotta version of the work is to be found in the Victoria and Albert Museum in London.

GIUSEPPE PIAMONTINI
Mary Magdalene

1720-1730
Silver
Height 30
Bronzes Inv. no. 884

Made in silver as a precious object for private devotion, this small sculpture was purchased recently for the Bargello collections by the Italian State.

The attribution to Giuseppe Piamontini is confirmed by the comparison of the drapery, garments and physical features with those of *Abraham's Sacrifice* (held in a private collection) and the *St Louis of France* in the Bronzes Room. The lustre of the silver highlights the elegance of the piece, the fine detail traced in the neobaroque forms of the "penitent" and the naturalistic aspects of the rock, the leaves and tufts of grass.

PISANELLO
Lionello d'Este,
Marquis of Ferrara

c. 1440

Bronze; diameter 6.7
General Inv. no. 5885

The medal bears around its border the inscription LEONELLUS MARCHIO ESTENSIS and on the back OPUS PISANI PICTORIS. It is considered to be the first in a series of seven medals made in Ferrara for Lionello d'Este in the mid 1440s. The image was reproduced by Giovanni Badile in a fresco in Santa Maria della Scala in Verona in 1443.

NICCOLÒ FIORENTINO
(MANNER OF)
Giovanna Albizzi

1485-1486

Bronze; diameter 7.5
General Inv. no. 6006

The medal is believed to have been made on the occasion of the marriage of Giovanna Albizzi with Lorenzo Tornabuoni (1486), and therefore prior to Ghirlandaio's posthumous portrait in Santa Maria Novella in Florence (1490).
The inscription on the back CASTITAS-PULCHRI-TUDO-AMOR, refers to "Beauty" according to Marsilio Ficino's Neoplatonic definition.

TULLIO LOMBARDO
Bust of Christ

1520

Marble; height 45
Sculpture Inv. no. 534

This work was donated to the Museum in 2001. It was previously in a German private collection and is attributed to Tullio Lombardo based on stylistic analogies with other works by the sculptor. Among the most pertinent, is the comparison with the figure of Christ in the centre of the *Coronation of the Virgin* in the Church of San Giovanni Grisostomo in Venice, signed, and dating to about 1500. Tullio Solari belonged to a family of sculptors called "Lombardo", originally from the Lombardy region, and principally active in Venice and the Veneto region. The back of the head is carefully sculpted while the same area of the bust is only partially worked. Framed by a short, well-trimmed beard, the facial expression seems serene, and the eyes are lowered. The marble is perfectly smoothed and finished, conveying a softness to the flesh. On the back of the bust the date "MDXX" and the letters "PB" are incised as well as a crest in the shape of a shield charged with a "B". The monogram is may be connected to the family of Pietro Bernardo or the Bembo family.

73

THE ARMOURY

The Armoury of the Bargello, which originated in the Grand-ducal collections, was established in 1865, along with the flags and a extremely picturesque nineteenth-century decor, in what is now the Michelangelo Room. After the flood of 1966, for security reasons, it was moved to this room (which previously housed Andrea del Castagno's Famous Men and Women *series). The Grand-ducal nucleus of the collection, originally in the Via Larga Palace, as a result of famous events, was moved to the Palazzo della Signoria, and was subsequently divided between the Armoury of Palazzo Vecchio, the secret armoury of Palazzo Pitti and that of the Uffizi. At the end of the 18th century – in line with the Illuminist climate of the time – 9,500 exemplars were sold off leaving only the nucleus which was considered historic; upon the creation of the Bargello this came to form part of the new Museum. In 1888 the Bargello Armoury was further enriched by the Carrand and Ressman bequests. The exemplars on display, produced with an exceptional technical skill in terms of both goldsmith's craft and pictorial art, include historical armours and war arms. Among the historical armours, connected with parades, tournaments, jousting and hunting (including examples from the Milan workshops of Filippo and Giovan Paolo Negroli, and the Mantua workshop of Modrone) are the* Cosimo I's Breastplate, *helmets (such as the* "Borgognotta" *with the dragon and the* Tournament *with visor), round shields (including those with* Samson and Delilah, The Medusa *and a rare, painted shield depicting* Venus and Cupid Riding Sea Monsters, *donated in 2002), precious cross-bows, sabres, rapiers, shields and the actual* Buratto *which was used in the Via Larga Saracen Joust. The so-called war-arms include visors, gauntlets, backplates, sollerets, cavalry armour, breastplates, daggers, halberds and swords, together with the later firearms.*

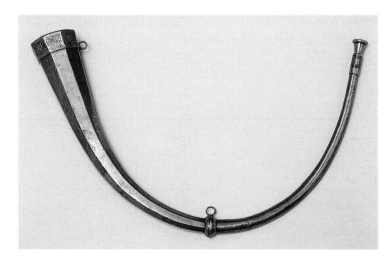

Hunting horn (Florence, 15th century)

NORTHERN ITALY
Cavalry armour

1565-1570
Steel
Height 110
Museum Armour
Inv. nos. 746, 751

In 1634 Vittoria della Rovere married the Gran Duke Ferdinand II de' Medici, and through this inheritance many of the Della Rovere works came into the Medici collections. This armour forms part of a collection of arms which passed to Florence on the death of Francesco Maria II, Duke of Urbino.

FILIPPO NEGROLI
Cosimo I's "Roman style" breastplate

c. 1546
Steel, gold
60×35×30
Museum Armour
Inv. nos. 768, 769

The technical and artistic skill revealed in this "Roman style" breastplate have led to its attribution to the armourer Filippo Negroli (with the possible collaboration of his brother Francesco in the gold touches), at the period of Cosimo I's nomination as Knight of the Golden Fleece.

75

NORTHERN ITALY
Parade saddle

1450-1470
Wood, partially painted
bone, staghorn, parchment
38.5 × 26.5 × 47
Ivories Inv. no. 3

This piece comes from the Medici collections and is mentioned for the first time in the 1631 Inventory of the Guardaroba. An even more detailed description, allowing for its identification, is found in the inventory from 1639 where it is paired with another so-called "muscovite" saddle. The wood structure is covered in parchment adorned with partially painted carved bone decorations. On the interior, it is covered with birch bark preventing the saddle from sticking to the sweaty hide of the horse. This type of saddle is very rare, and is characterised by the presence of saddle-bows, differentiating it from a "muscovite" saddle which did not have this element.

A "muscovite" saddle, again from the Medici collections, is in the Museum's possession and is listed in the 1639 Inventory. The saddle is covered in bone reliefs depicting individual or paired young men dressed in fifteenth-century costume, young girls and angels holding scrolls with inscriptions (ASPETO TEMPO, AMOR, LAUS DEO), fight scenes with dragons and lions. The background is covered with foliage and cloud-filled skies from which tongues of fire descend. On the back of the rear saddle-bow there are two dragons facing each other, placed on either side of a wreath centred with a crest, now lost.

These types of saddles where used in tournaments and parades, and were fashionable in Germanic countries and in Italy until the 1500s.

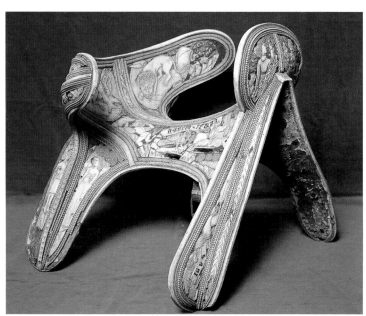

ITALY
Ceremonial "Borgognotta" Helmet

1450-1475

Steel, gilded copper
52×35×26
Museum Armour
Inv. no. 782

A result of the combination of a sixteenth-century borgognotta with a fifteenth-century crest, in engraved and gilded copper, terminating in the beak of an eagle with spread wings. It is considered that this later reconstruction served a similar function in the Florentine tournaments of the Medici period.

GASPARO MOLA
Parade "Borgognotta" Helmet

1608-1609

Steel, gilded copper, silver
36×34×23
Museum Armour Inv. no. 761

The activity of Gasparo Mola as an armour decorator is recorded only at the Medici Court. This exemplar, which together with its shield formed part of the equipment for the game of borgognotta, was already recorded in 1631 as 'an infantry helmet made on a base of iron... with brass foliage and grotesque shapes worked as on the said shield'.

INDEX